FIRST FESTIVALS

Christmas

Lois Rock

CPH
SAINT LOUIS

Introduction

This edition published by
Concordia Publishing House
3558 S. Jefferson Avenue
St. Louis, MO 63118-3968
ISBN 0 570 07190 9

Text copyright © 2001 Lion Publishing
Illustrations copyright © 1999 Helen Cann
Music arrangements copyright © 1998 Philip Tebbs,
typeset by MSS Studios, Gwynedd
Photography by John Williams Studios, Thame
Text and artefacts by Lois Rock

First published by
Lion Publishing plc
Sandy Lane West, Oxford, England
www.lion-publishing.co.uk
ISBN 0 7459 3907 4

1 2 3 4 5 6 7 8 9 10   10 09 08 07 06 05 04 03 02 01

Printed and bound in Singapore

Acknowledgments
Scriptures quoted from the Good News Bible published by The
Bible Societies/HarperCollins Publishers Ltd, UK © American
Bible Society 1966, 1971, 1976, 1992, used with permission.

This book is part of a series featuring Christian festivals. It is about the best-loved of them all: the celebration of Christmas.

Here you will find traditional crafts to mark the season—from Advent preparations to Christmas Day itself, with its gifts, cards, and decorations.

May this book help you and your family focus your celebrations around Jesus, the Savior, who lies at the heart of Christmas. Enjoy learning more about the carols that sing out the story of Jesus' birth and Christian traditions that have shaped the customs of the season.

Contents

Advent

As wintertime grows cold and bleak, Christians begin a time of preparation for a celebration that is full of light, warmth, and joy.

This season of preparation is called "Advent." It comes from a Latin word that means "coming." Advent begins four Sundays before Christmas and focuses on the coming of the Savior. We use the time during Advent to get our hearts and our houses ready to welcome Jesus.

Advent is also about promises. Bible readings focus on God's promise to send a Savior from sin and the Old Testament prophesies that foretell the birth of the long-awaited King.

A promise of a king

The people who walked in darkness have seen a great light.
They lived in a land of shadows, but now light is shining on them.
A child is born to us!
A Son is given to us!
And He will be our ruler.
He will be called "Wonderful Counselor," "Mighty God," "Eternal Father,"
   "Prince of Peace."
His royal power will continue to grow; His kingdom will always be at peace.

(Isaiah 9:2, 6–7)

2 Advent Ring

The ring, or wreath, is a tradition associated with Advent. The four candles count the Sundays that lead to Christmas.

On the first Sunday, one candle is lit. As it burns, the family can read passages from the Bible to remind them of God's promise to send a Savior from sin.

On the second Sunday, light two candles; on the third, light three; and on the fourth, light four.

On Christmas Day, the Christ candle in the center is lit as the family remembers the birth of the Savior— "Christ," the baby Jesus.

You will need

large garden saucer

damp soil or sand

5 small flowerpots

4 blue or purple candles

1 tall white candle

sprigs of evergreens such as fir, holly, or ivy

1 Fill the garden saucer with soil or sand. Wedge four flowerpots in a circle around the edge, and another in the center. Fill these half full with soil or sand.

2 Put the blue (or purple) candles in the pots around the edge. Add the white candle to the pot in the center.

3 Push evergreen sprigs into the sand to cover it. Take care to keep the leaves below the rim of the pots, so they will not catch fire as the candles burn.

3 Advent Calendar

An Advent calendar helps count the days to Christmas. This one, like many, counts from December 1st to Christmas Day, December 25th. Often there is a hidden surprise for every day in Advent.

1 Draw a simple Christmas tree shape. This sample is 28 inches tall including the pot. Ask a grown-up to help you cut it out, using a craft knife against a ruler on a cutting mat.

2 Mark equally spaced lines to show where the yarn will go. Cut notches where these lines meet the edge of the tree.

3 Paint the tree green and the pot red. Let dry.

4 Wind fuzzy yarn around the tree, using the notches as guides. Add tape on the back of the poster board to hold the beginning and end of the yarn in place.

You will need

large sheet of poster board

pencil and ruler

cutting mat and craft knife

green and red acrylic paint

paintbrushes

fuzzy yarn

tape

This Advent calendar is shaped like a Christmas tree. Each plain envelope contains a paper decoration. Unwrap one decoration each day and hang it on the tree.

Make an extra special star to put on the top for Christmas Day. Use tape, yarn, or sticky putty to hold it in place.

4 Decorations

Here's how to make bright decorations and envelopes for your Advent calendar tree.

Decorations

You will need

card stock

pencil

scissors

construction paper

colored yarn

tape

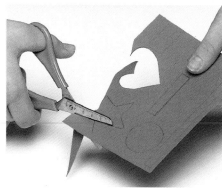

1 Draw shapes like the ones shown here onto card stock. Cut them out. Use the templates at the back of this book as guides.

2 One at a time, hold a shape against a piece of construction paper and tear it, little by little, along the edges to get the same shape. Tear out the shapes you need to make 25 decorations!

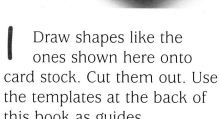

3 Glue the shapes together to make decorations.

4 Cut yarn in 6-inch lengths and fold each in half. Tape a piece of yarn to each decoration on the wrong side, with the cut ends free so you can tie the decoration onto your tree.

Envelopes

You will need

large sheets of red paper

gold paper clips

ruler and pencil

scissors

gold pen

gold stickers

1 Use a ruler and pencil to mark squares on the red paper. The squares for the envelopes shown here are 4 inches x 4 inches.

2 Place a ruler along each line. Tear the paper firmly along the edge of the ruler. First tear the marked paper into strips. Then tear the strips into mini squares.

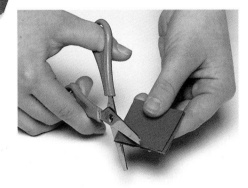

3 Fold each square in half, then in half again. Hold the folded paper with the center point toward you, and snip a tiny piece off the two side corners but not the top one.

4 Unfold it. There will be a notch in the middle of each side. Lay your decoration in the middle of the square. Then fold in each point over it, folding from notch to notch.

5 Sticker the envelope shut to hold the points together.

6 Number each envelope from 1 to 25. Hang them on the tree in order, from the bottom of the tree to the top, using a paper clip on the yarn (see the picture on page 3).

5 The Christmas Story

At the heart of Christmas is the story of the birth of Jesus, our Savior. The account of this wonderful story is found in the Bible in Luke 1:26–28 and Luke 2:1-20. Read this story together.

Mary and the angel

Long ago, in the town of Nazareth in Palestine, lived a young woman named Mary. Like all the girls her age, she was planning to get married. The man who was going to be her husband was named Joseph.

One day, an angel appeared to Mary. "Greetings," said the angel. "I bring special news. God has chosen you to bear a child—the king

for whom your people are waiting. You are to call him Jesus."

Mary was puzzled and dismayed. "How can I be a mother?" she asked. "I'm not yet a wife!"

"God will make this happen," said the angel. Mary felt blessed to do God's will.

The birth of Jesus

Months went by. The time was coming when Mary's baby would be born. An announcement came from the emperor who ruled the land. He wanted to know exactly how many people lived in his empire, so he could ask them to pay taxes. Everyone was ordered to go to their hometown to put their names on a list.

So Joseph took Mary from Nazareth to Bethlehem. Many people were traveling for the same reason. In crowded Bethlehem, the only place where Mary and Joseph could find shelter was a stable.

There, the baby was born. Mary wrapped the child in swaddling clothes and laid Him in a manger.

Away in a Manger

A - way in a — man-ger, no — crib for a bed, The —

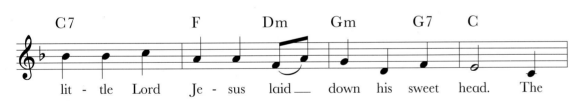

lit - tle Lord Je - sus laid — down his sweet head. The

stars in the — bright sky looked — down where he lay, The —

lit - tle Lord Je - sus a - sleep on the hay.

The cattle are lowing, the baby awakes,
But little Lord Jesus, no crying He makes.
I love Thee, Lord Jesus! Look down from the sky,
And stay by my side until morning is nigh.

Be near me, Lord Jesus, I ask Thee to stay
Close by me forever, and love me, I pray.
Bless all the dear children in Thy tender care,
And take us to heaven to live with Thee there.

The shepherds on the hillside

On the same night that God's Son was born, there were some shepherds out on the hillside near Bethlehem. They were watching over their sheep.

Suddenly, an angel appeared. The shepherds were terrified.

"Do not be afraid," said the angel. "I bring you good news, and the good news is for everyone. Tonight, a Savior has been born in the town of Bethlehem. He is Christ the Lord. You will find the baby wrapped in swaddling clothes and lying in a manger."

Then a great crowd of angels appeared. They sang songs of praise:

"Glory to God in the highest, and peace on earth to men."

When the angels had gone, the shepherds looked at one another in amazement.

"Let us go to Bethlehem, and see what has happened," they said.

So they went, and they found Mary and the baby, just as the angel had said.

While Shepherds Watched Their Flocks

While shep - herds watched their flocks by night, All

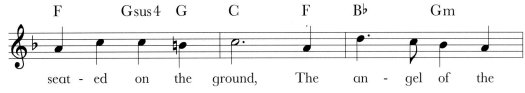

seat - ed on the ground, The an - gel of the

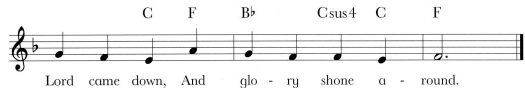

Lord came down, And glo - ry shone a - round.

"Fear not," said he, for mighty dread
Had seized their troubled mind;
"Glad tidings of great joy I bring
To you and all mankind.

"To you in David's town this day
Is born of David's line
A Savior who is Christ the Lord;
And this shall be the sign:

"The heavenly Babe you there shall find
To human view displayed,
All meanly wrapped in swaddling clothes,
And in a manger laid."

Thus spake the seraph and forthwith
Appeared a shining throng
Of angels praising God, who thus
Addressed their joyful song:

"All glory be to God on high,
And on the earth be peace;
Goodwill henceforth from heaven to men
Begin and never cease."

7 The Christmas Story

The wise men

When Jesus was born in Bethlehem, a man named Herod was king. His palace was in the nearby city of Jerusalem.

Some men who studied the stars came to Jerusalem from lands to the east. They had an important question for the people there: "Where is the baby who is born to be your king? We have seen His star and have come to worship Him."

King Herod heard of their search and became angry. He hated anyone who threatened his power. So he called together his chief priests and teachers. "You have studied the ancient writings of our people," he said. "They tell us that one day God will send us a special king—the Christ. Where will the Christ be born?"

"In Bethlehem," they replied.

Then Herod called the travelers from the east to a secret meeting, and asked them what they knew about the star and when they had first seen it. When he had found out all they knew, he sent them to Bethlehem.

"Search for the king there," he told them. "Then come back and tell me where He is."

So the men left. They followed the star until it stopped right over the place where Jesus was. They went in and found the newborn king with His mother Mary.

They worshipped Jesus and presented the gifts they had brought: gold, and frankincense, and myrrh.

Then they went back to their own land. In a dream, God told them not to go back to Herod, so they chose a different way home.

We Three Kings

We three kings of O - ri - ent are; Bear - ing gifts we

tra - vel a - far. Field and foun - tain, moor and moun - tain,

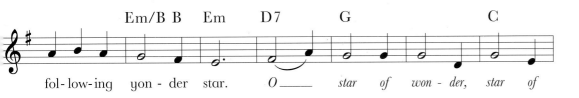

fol - low - ing yon - der star. O ___ star of won - der, star of

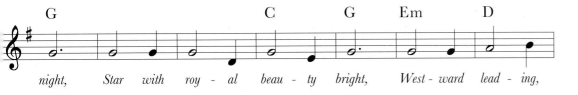

night, Star with roy - al beau - ty bright, West - ward lead - ing,

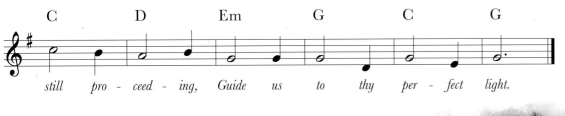

still pro - ceed - ing, Guide us to thy per - fect light.

Melchior:
Born a king on Bethlehem plain,
Gold I bring to crown Him again,
King for ever, ceasing never
Over us all to reign. *(Chorus)*

Caspar:
Frankincense to offer have I,
Incense owns a deity nigh;
Prayer and praising, all men raising,
Worship Him, God most high!
(Chorus)

Balthazar:
Myrrh is mine, its bitter perfume
Breathes a life of gathering gloom;
Sorrowing, sighing, bleeding, dying,
Sealed in the stone-cold tomb.
(Chorus)

Glorious now behold Him arise,
King and God and sacrifice,
Alleluia, alleluia,
Earth to the heavens replies. *(Chorus)*

8 A Nativity Scene

The Christmas story of the birth of Jesus is often called the nativity, which means "birth." Some people act out the story in nativity plays at Christmas. Some set up a model of what happened in the story—a nativity scene.

A stable

You will need

cardboard box

craft knife or strong scissors

white glue

white and brown acrylic paints

paintbrushes

straight twigs

strip of clear acetate film (overhead projector film is good)

gold card

tape

pencil

3 Color in the hands, feet, and head. Color the back and the front.

4 Open up the figure shape and place double-sided tape on the inside along the arms and head. Fold the figure right-side-out and press the tape to stick the top of the figure together.

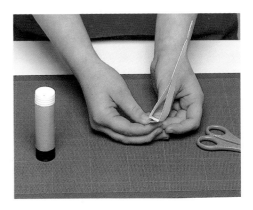

5 Fold the tabs at the bottom of each figure inward and overlap them. Glue them together to make a base that will allow the figure to stand upright.

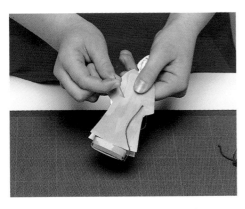

8 Add extra details if you wish. The belt is made by stitching a piece of yarn through the figure at waist level and tying a knot. The angel's wings are cut from a doily and taped to the back.

9 Make a manger from brown paper. Cut a rectangle 3 inches x 2 inches and fold in 1/2 inch along each side. Make snips as shown along the long creases to where they cross the short creases.

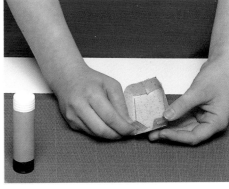

10 Fold in the sides and glue in place. Fill the manger with straw made from snipped paper. Add a baby that you have drawn on thin card stock and cut out.

10 Christmas Gifts

The New Testament is filled with true stories about Jesus. He taught many people about God the Father and His love. He taught that the God who made the world is kind, loving, and forgiving. He taught people to love God and to be kind and forgiving to everyone around them. Many people listened to what Jesus had to say. And many people have asked God to help them live as Jesus taught. Here is the legend of one such man.

The story of Saint Nicholas

Long ago, in the town of Myra, lived a man named Nicholas. He was the leader of the Christian community, and everyone knew him as a good and generous man.

In the town lived a poor family with three daughters. They were all old enough to get married. However, it was the tradition that a bride must bring a gift of money to her new family… and their father had none. No one wanted to marry them, and they were very sad.

Nicholas heard of their sorrow.

He gathered together some gold coins. One dark night, he crept up to where the sisters lived, and threw the coins in through an open window.

The coins landed by the hearth, where the sisters had left their wet clothes to dry. In the morning, they found gold coins among their shoes and stockings—gifts that would enable them to get married and live happily.

It is said that Nicholas did many kind deeds like this. Some people even began to call him a saint: Saint Nicholas (or Santa Claus)!

To this day many people hang up stockings on Christmas Eve, and on Christmas morning find that they have been filled with good things by a gift-giver who comes in secret.

11 Stockings

Here are some Christmas stockings to decorate.

Where will you hang your stocking? Do you think you will find it full of gifts on Christmas morning?

Will you be a gift-giver and help fill a stocking secretly for someone you love?

You will need

long socks in bright colors

bright yarn, buttons, and beads

tapestry needle

Thread the needle with your first choice of bright yarn. Pull the two ends even. Push the needle through the folded cuff at a place where you want to place a tuft.

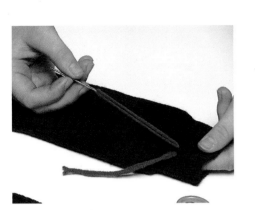

2 Take care to keep your other hand in the opening, so you don't stitch the opening up! Pull the needle through, leaving a tail of yarn about 4 inches long on the right side.

3 Cut the thread to leave another tail about 4 inches long on the left side.

4 Tie the ends with a reef knot: Wind the right thread over the left and pull snugly. Then wind left over right and pull tight.

5 Snip the tails to leave a tuft about 3/4 inch long. Make tufts over the entire cuff in your choice of colors.

6 Use the same method to tie beads or buttons on your stocking. Work from the inside out and, using a single piece of yarn, thread through a bead or button before taking the needle back to the inside. Tie off the ends on the inside and snip them about 3/4 inch long.

12 The Christmas Tree

Decorating a tree with lights and ornaments is a favorite Christmas tradition. Here is one story about how the tradition began.

The child and the fir tree

It is said that long ago, a man named Boniface set off through Europe on a special journey. In the lands where he was traveling, people had never heard the story of Jesus. They did not believe in a God of love and gentleness. Some of the customs they followed were harsh and cruel.

One night, Boniface came across a gathering in the forest. People stood around a mighty oak tree. Tied to its trunk was a frightened child.

"What is going on?" Boniface wanted to know.

"The child must be offered as a sacrifice to our gods," came the answer.

Boniface was dismayed. "Please wait," he said. "I believe that the great God of heaven and earth does not want this child to be killed. I want to tell you about Jesus, God's Son, who came to earth to save the world from sin and demonstrate the love of God."

What he said made the people change their minds. When they had finished listening, they allowed Boniface to untie the child. They agreed to cut the oak tree down.

By its roots was a little fir tree. "The oak that you used for your old customs is gone," he said. "This tree is a symbol of your new belief as followers of Jesus."

13 Gingerbread Hearts

These simple tree decorations are spicy cookies. Their heart shape and their sweetness are a reminder of the love people can show one another.

Christmas is a time to remember that Jesus told His followers to love one another.

You will need

1/3 c brown sugar

2 T light corn syrup

1 T molasses

1 T water

7 T margarine

1 tsp cinnamon

1 tsp ginger

1 c plus 2 T self-rising flour

extra flour

2 bowls

mixing spoon

rolling pin

drinking straws

baking parchment

heart-shaped cookie cutters

cookie sheets

wire rack

yarn

☺ Ask a grown-up to help you preheat the oven to 325°F.

☺ Always wash your hands before cooking.

1 Put the sugar, syrup, molasses, water, and margarine into a bowl. Microwave on high for 2 minutes. Stir and microwave for 1 minute more.

5 Put a large sheet of baking parchment on a clean work surface. Sprinkle some extra flour on it. Roll the dough to 1/4 inch thick with a rolling pin.

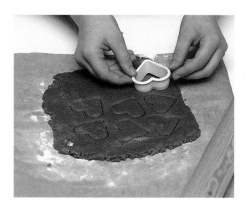

6 Line a cookie sheet with baking parchment. Use a heart-shaped cutter to cut out your cookies. Lay them on the lined cookie sheet.

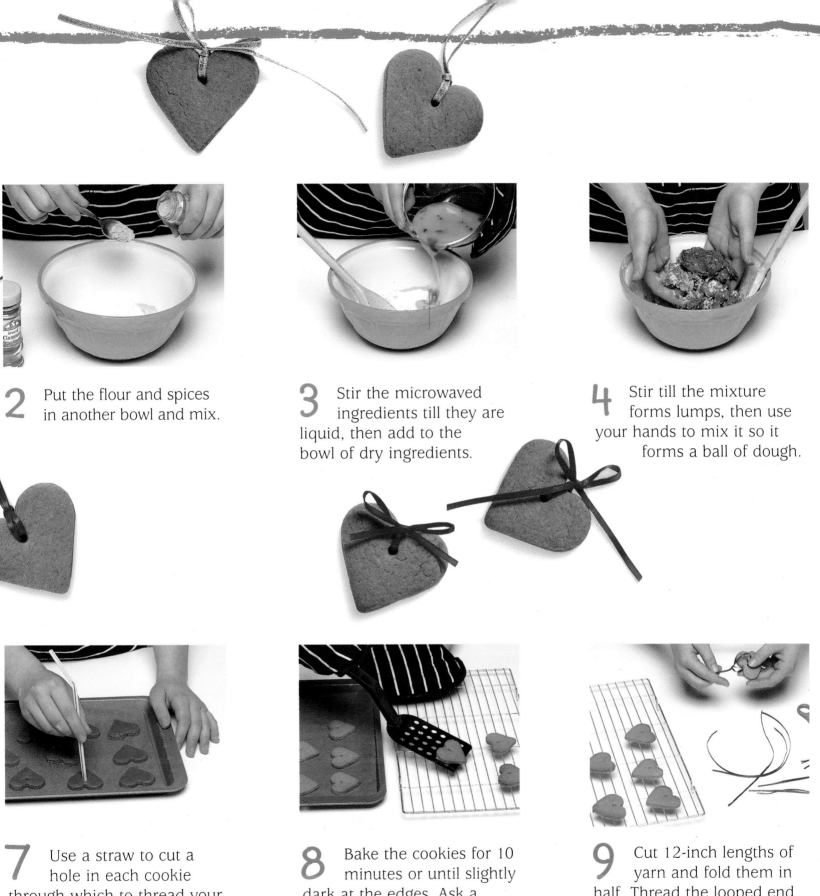

2 Put the flour and spices in another bowl and mix.

3 Stir the microwaved ingredients till they are liquid, then add to the bowl of dry ingredients.

4 Stir till the mixture forms lumps, then use your hands to mix it so it forms a ball of dough.

7 Use a straw to cut a hole in each cookie through which to thread your hanging loop. Press the end into the cookie and twist it slightly to lift out the tiny circle of dough (which will be pushed up into the straw).

8 Bake the cookies for 10 minutes or until slightly dark at the edges. Ask a grown-up to lift them out of the oven and leave them on the cookie sheet till firm. Then lift them onto a wire rack to finish cooling.

9 Cut 12-inch lengths of yarn and fold them in half. Thread the looped end through the hanging hole of each heart, and then thread the dangling end through this loop. Use the ends to tie the cookie onto the tree.

14 Woven Hearts

These woven paper hearts can be another decoration. The colors chosen here stand for heaven and earth—a reminder that Jesus was God's Son, come from heaven to show God's love on earth.

You will need

thick card stock

pencil and ruler

colored paper

scissors

needle and yarn

1 Copy the shape shown at the back of this book onto thick card stock and cut it out. Mark the center line as shown. Snip each side of the line and remove the thin curl of card in the middle.

2 Fold the colored paper in half, wrong side showing. Lay the thick card stock with the flat end exactly on the crease. Draw around it. Mark the center line as well.

5 Next hold the folded end of the right-hand strip as you pull it through. Open up the fold and loop the strip over the upper strip of the left-hand shape.

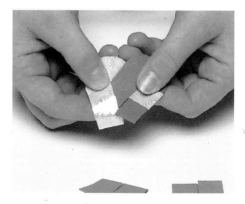

6 Push the right-hand piece down so it settles into the slit on the left for the second part of the weaving. Take the top strip of the right-hand shape, open up the folded edge, and loop it over the strip on the left.

3 Cut out the colored shape and snip ONCE along the center line. Make shapes in different colors. Refold each one with right-side-out.

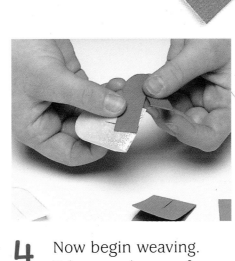

4 Now begin weaving. Take two shapes of different colors and hold one in each hand with the folded ends facing out. Push the lower strip of the shape in your right hand in between the two layers of the strip in your left.

7 Next, fold the edge of the right-hand strip closed again and push it through the left-hand shape. Jiggle the paper so the weaving fits snugly.

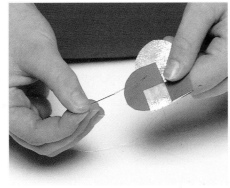

8 Thread a hanging loop through all thicknesses.

Many people send Christmas cards to tell their family and friends that they love and remember them.

1 On card stock measure a rectangle as tall as the size of card you want and three times as wide. Cut it out, using a craft knife against a ruler on a cutting mat.

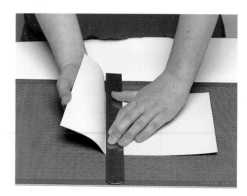

2 Mark the card into three panels along the top and bottom edges. Lay the ruler on the card to join them, and score lightly down this line with the craft knife. Fold the card along this line, keeping the ruler in place to make the creases straight.

You will need

strong tracing paper or clear acetate film

stick of repositionable glue

craft knife and cutting mat

pencil and ruler

colored card stock

acrylic paint

stencil brushes

block of polystyrene

thick needle

thin needle and thread

double-sided sticky tape

beads

scrap paper

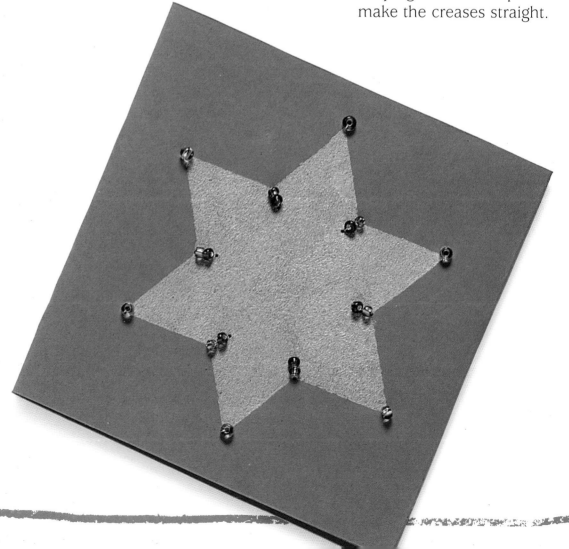

3 Draw a stencil design for your card on the tracing paper or acetate film. Cut out the stencil design using the craft knife on the cutting mat.

4 Spread a little glue on the back of the stencil, then lay it on the middle panel of the card where you want the design to go. Put some paint on a saucer and dab the stencil brush in it. Dab paint on the stencil hole, taking care not to damage the edges of the stencil.

5 Peel the stencil away and let the card dry. Blot the back of the stencil on scrap paper before using it to make other cards in the same way.

6 Decide where you want to put beads on the card—like the glittery beads that add sparkle to the star, or the decorations on the tree. Open up the card and lay it on the polystyrene block. Use the thick needle to make holes where the beads will go.

7 Thread a thinner needle and tape the end of the thread on the inside of the card near a hole. Bring the needle to the front through a hole, pick up a bead, and take the needle back through the hole. Take the needle to the next hole and do the same till all the holes have beads. Tape the end of the thread firmly on the inside.

8 Fold the front panel of the card inward so it covers the back of the middle panel. Tape it in place with double-sided tape.

16 Christmas News

The Good News of Jesus' birth is too wonderful to keep secret. Here is a Christmas carol that encourages you to tell others that Christ the Savior has been born.

Go, Tell It on the Mountain

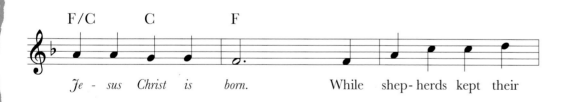

(Chorus)
And lo, when they had seen it,
They all bowed down and prayed,
They travelled on together
To where the babe was laid.
(Chorus)

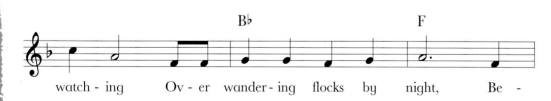

17 Gift Wrapping

You can hide any gift in this clever bag.

You will need

scissors

wrapping paper

tape

hole punch

gift ribbon

gift, loosely wrapped in tissue paper

1 Cut a rectangle of wrapping paper large enough to go loosely around the gift, with extra at the top and bottom.

2 Lay the paper wrong side up and fold the sides so they overlap in the middle. Tape at the joint and crease the side edges firmly.

6 Unfold the top and put the gift inside. Then refold the top and tape shut.

7 Taking care not to damage the gift inside, punch a hole in each corner of the bag.

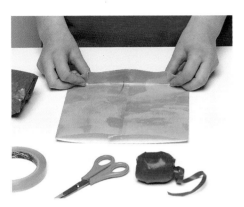

3 Fold a small triangle in at each of the bottom corners, then fold the lower edge up. Tape in place.

4 Now open up the top of the bag and bring the side creases together. Crease the new sides a few inches down from the top.

5 Fold triangles in on these new sides, then fold down the top edge. Crease firmly but do not tape.

8 Thread ribbon through each hole and tie a knot. Tie it into bows or curl it.

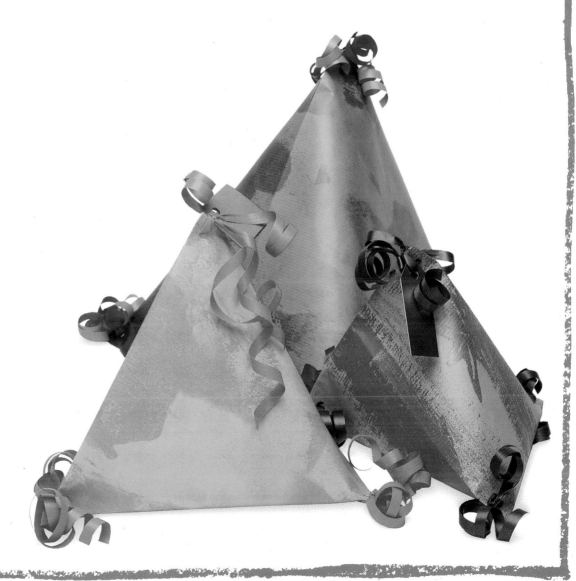

Just think of all the ways you can wrap gifts to make them look really festive.

It's a good idea to add a tag to each gift, saying who it is for and who it is from.

1 Cut a simple shape from bright card.

2 Punch a hole in the tag.

You will need

bright card

scissors

hole punch

gift ribbon

pen

3 Add your message.

4 Tie the tag to the gift wrap.

We Wish You a Merry Christmas

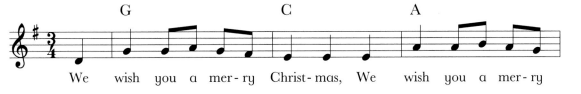

We wish you a mer-ry Christ-mas, We wish you a mer-ry

Christ-mas, We wish you a mer-ry Christ-mas And a hap-py New

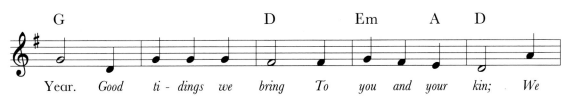

Year. *Good ti-dings we bring To you and your kin; We*

wish you a mer-ry Christ-mas And a hap-py New Year.

Now bring us some figgy pudding,
Now bring us some figgy pudding,
Now bring us some figgy pudding,
And bring some out here. *(Chorus)*

For we all like figgy pudding,
We all like figgy pudding,
We all like figgy pudding,
So bring some out here. *(Chorus)*

And we won't go till we've got some,
We won't go till we've got some,
We won't go till we've got some,
So bring some out here. *(Chorus)*

19 Christingle

The Christingle is a traditional Christmas gift from around the world. Some churches (especially in England) have special services at which Christingles are given to children and everyone sings carols as the candles burn.

The different parts of the Christingle help tell the story of Jesus.

The **orange** stands for the world God made.

The **sweets and fruits** stand for the people in all the four corners of the world.

The **red ribbon** stands for forgiveness. It is red like the color of Jesus' blood. Jesus came to earth as our Savior. He lived a perfect life, then died on the cross for the forgiveness of our sins. He rose again on Easter. Because of Jesus, our sins are forgiven. Because of Jesus, all believers will have eternal life in heaven.

The **candle** stands for Jesus, who is the Light of the world— shining the light of God's love for all to see.

You will need

an orange

double-sided tape

red ribbon

scissors

4 cocktail toothpicks

sweets and fruits

apple corer

aluminum foil

candle

1 Wrap the double-sided tape around the middle of the orange.

2 Unpeel the backing and stick the ribbon in place on top of it. Tie a small knot to hold the ribbon tight and trim the ends.

3 Use the corer to make a candle-sized hole in the top of the orange.

4 Skewer sweets and fruits on the toothpicks and stick them into the orange.

5 Wrap foil around the bottom of the candle and push it firmly into the orange.

The story of the very first Christmas is the story of Jesus' birth. Its message is clear: that God loved the world so much that He sent a Savior (read John 3:16).

Bright paper chains link many different colors. They can be a reminder at Christmas of how many different kinds of people are joined together in God's love.

1 With ruler and pencil, mark strips 1 inch x 6 inches on your paper.

2 Lay the ruler along the line and pull upward on the paper to tear it into strips 6 inches wide. Lay the ruler on the other lines to tear off strips 1 inch wide. Make strips in different colors.

3 Take one strip and tape it into a circle.

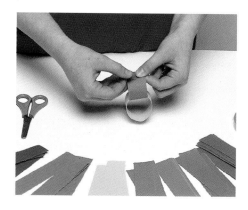

4 Thread another strip through it and tape that into a circle. Add more strips to make your chain as long as you like.

Paper chains

You will need

colored paper

ruler and pencil

tape

A Christmas prayer

God, our loving Father, help us remember the birth of Jesus, that we may share in the song of the angels, the gladness of the shepherds, and the wisdom of the Wise Men.

Close the door of hate and open the door of love all over the world.

Let kindness come with every gift and good desires with every greeting.

Deliver us from evil by the blessing which Christ brings and teach us to be merry with clean hearts.

May the Christmas morning make us happy to be Your children and the Christmas evening bring us to our beds with grateful thoughts, forgiving and forgiven, for Jesus' sake. Amen.

Robert Louis Stevenson (1850–94)

templates for Nativity characters on page 9

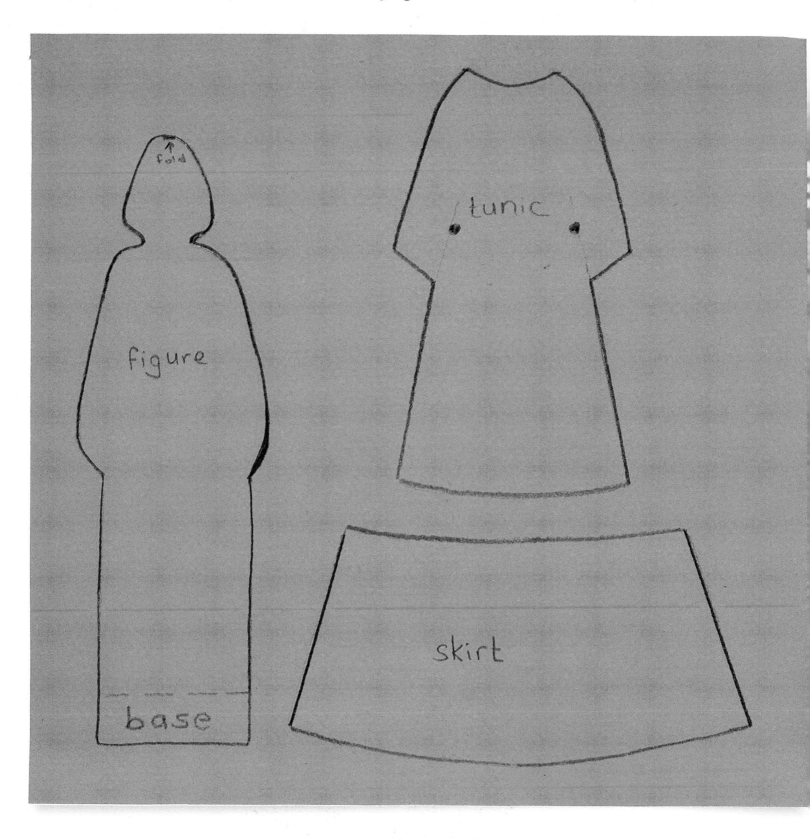